OMNIBUS PRESS
LONDON/NEW YORK/SYDNEY

Edited by Chris Charlesworth
Book designed by Pearce Marchbank, Studio Twenty
Computer management by Adam Hay Editorial Design
Picture research by David Brolan

Exclusive Distributors:
Book Sales Limited
8-9 Frith Street
London W1V 5TZ, UK
Music Sales Corporation
257 Park Avenue South
New York, NY 10010, USA
Music Sales Pty Limited
120 Rothschild Avenue, Rosebery
NSW 2018, Australia
To the Music Trade only:
Music Sales Limited
8-9, Frith Street
London W1V 5TZ, UK

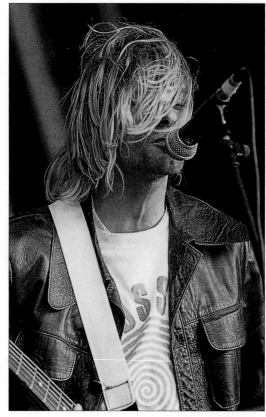

Photographs by:
David Anderson/SIN: 22-23, 26
George Chin: 8-9, 27
Steve Double: 20-21,24, 25
Frank Forcino/LFI: 18-19, 48
Martyn Goodacre/SIN: 3, 14
Mick Hutson/Redferns: 36-37
Alastair Indge/Retna: 12-13
Michael Lavine/Katz: 1
Ian Lawton/SIN: 37, 40-41
Michel Linssen/Redferns: 32, 28, 29, 42
Kevin Mazur/LFI: 16, 30-31
Frank Micelotta/Katz: front cover
Phil Nicholls/LFI: 31
Phil Nicholls/SIN: 11
Frank W Ockenfels/Katz: back cover
Charles Peterson: 7
Ebet Roberts/Redferns: 45
Ed Sirrs/Retna: back cover,
4-5, 14-15, 42-43, 44-45
Geoff Swaine/LFI: 2, 6, 34, 35
Stephen Sweet/Retna: 17, 33
Justin Thomas/All Action: 9
Ian T Tilton/SIN: 38, 39, 47

OMNIBUS PRESS
Copyright © 1994 Omnibus Press
(A Division of Book Sales Limited)
ISBN 0.7119.4244.7
Order No. OP47696

Every effort has been made to trace the
copyright holders of the photographs in this
book but one or two were unreachable.
We would be grateful if the photographers
concerned would contact us.

Printed and bound in Great Britain.

HIS WORK MOTIVATED AND ENTERTAINED MILLIONS OF PEOPLE ACROSS THE GLOBE

WHAT THE HELL WAS HAPPENING WITH NIRVANA THIS WEEK?

The lanky frame of Chris Novoselic looks across the stage and watches as a battered wheelchair is pushed up to the microphone. In it sits the scrawny frame of his band's vocalist and guitarist, Kurt Cobain, wrapped in a white gown and wearing a blond wig. The roars of the 40,000 fans who've been waiting all weekend for this moment turn into mumbles of bewilderment. He'll be alright with the help of his family and friends, says Novoselic. The singer struggles to rise, clutching the arms of the chair, forcing himself up. With his guitar strapped precariously around him he sings one line of a song, then collapses on the floor, motionless. After a few seconds pause, he stands up, smiles, whips off the wig and launches into 'Breed'.

He is okay after all and the sense of relief is enormous. For three days Reading Festival has been immersed in yet another dramatic episode of the ongoing Nirvana saga. Would they appear? Were they still together as a band? Had Cobain overdosed? Was he still seeing his wife, Courtney Love? What the hell was happening with Nirvana *this week*? These and many other questions raced through the minds of all those who stood ankle deep in the cold, muddy Berkshire field, waiting for a performance by the most important band of the decade.

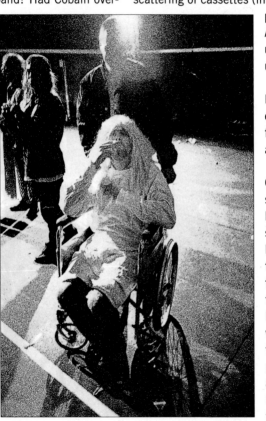

Fast forward to eighteen months later, to a private hospital in Rome. The singer lies in a drug and alcohol induced coma, while the world's media camps outside, speculating on his bruised body and troubled mind. Five days later he is on a plane, heading for Seattle and his baby daughter Frances Bean, Nirvana's European tour abruptly cancelled.

A month later he is dead, his life ended by a single gunshot wound to the head, alone, depressed, in his family home. Within hours of Kurt's suicide, the rumour mongers, tabloid hacks and genuine fans had gathered *en masse* around Washington East Boulevard. As the brisk morning passed into a mild afternoon, details began to filter through in greater clarity.

At 8.45am an electrician had called to do security work on the $1.1 million house into which the Cobains had moved in January. In the self-contained cottage above the family garage, where a grey Volvo was parked, he noticed something suspicious through a glass panel in the door frame. At first he thought it was a mannequin; then he saw dried blood trickling from the right ear and thought again. The sparsely furnished room was virtually empty but for the body of a white male, dressed in Converse boots, jeans and a thrift store shirt, lying in the corner, with a shotgun across his chest pointing at his chin.

When the police arrived on the scene, Kurt Cobain was certified dead, and his body removed for formal identification. Due to the severity of the facial injuries this had to be concluded on fingerprint evidence only. The District Coroner drove off down Lake Washington Boulevard, taking with him the body of a tortured mind, and with it the hopes and focus of a thousand like-minded kids across America and the world.

Sketchy details of the last days of Kurt's life came through and left many questions unanswered, and many questions still to be asked. The only irrefutable fact was that there would never be another record by Nirvana, the unlikely trio who had set out to break free of their insular home community of Aberdeen and taken the world along with them. The body was found early in the morning of April 8. There was a television switched on in the other side of the house but otherwise the property was silent. The room where Cobain was found had been used as a makeshift greenhouse so it was bare except for a handful of plants. Next to the singer's body was an ID card, a scattering of cassettes (including a copy of 'In Utero'), a computer game and a green cuddly toy. Alongside was a note, stuck into an upturned flower pot with the pen used to write it.

On the paper was scratched a lengthy message in red ink. All the electrician could make out was the final "I love you, I love you" farewell at the bottom of the page.

The following day on MTV, Courtney Love made her first public statement about the tragedy, stating briefly that she believed Kurt would still have been alive if someone had been with him during his darkest thoughts. By now the attraction of the spectacle had proved too great for fans to resist and the street had been cordoned off to prevent chaos, while MTV set up a counselling line for distressed fans. In LA, KROQ played Nirvana albums back to back all day. The following evening at the Seattle Flag Pavilion, 5,000 fans from early teens to middle age turned up for a candle-lit vigil in the singer's memory, while across town on the outskirts of the city a private ceremony was attended by 200 of Cobain's close friends and immediate family at The Holy Unity Church of Truth. After the resident minister spoke, Chris Novoselic read a brief tribute to his friend and colleague. Then Love, dressed entirely in black, told anecdotes about her husband and read extracts of his favourite poetry and passages from The Bible. Finally Danny Goldberg, the band's manager, added a small, but telling epitaph to the proceedings when he said, "I believe he would have left this world several years ago if he hadn't met Courtney."

Across town, at the public vigil, a taped message from Courtney Love, recorded at home on the bed she shared with her dead husband, was played over loud speakers. In a faltering voice, fraught with pain and emotion, Love read out the words of what she later called "the sweetest note" to the silent,

'LOOK ON THE BRIGHT SIDE IS SUICIDE'
'MILK IT' FROM 'IN UTERO'

stunned crowd. "He left a note for you," she said. "It's more like a letter to the editor." Halfway through she called her husband 'an asshole' for what he had done and urged those present to do the same, and she contradicted his assertion that to fake playing his music was the biggest crime he could commit. "No," she cried. "The worst crime is leaving!"

Her tearful, angry tone made for highly emotional listening, especially when she concluded by telling the congregation that the personal details were "none of your fucking business". This was followed by tributes from local radio luminaries and Cobain's uncle. Several Nirvana songs were then played across the Centre, including 'Heart Shaped Box' while fans waded into a fountain, cheered on by the crowd. Inflated condoms, balloons, burning candles and pictures of Cobain were scattered everywhere. Love herself appeared later, showing the note to close friends and accepting condolences from selected mourners. She said she had cut off a lock of her husband's blond hair and returned home to wash it fastidiously, something he had always hated doing.

Later, the full transcription of the note would become known. In it Cobain attempted to explain the despair that had driven him to this extreme measure. "I haven't felt the music or written anything for years now," he wrote. "I haven't felt the excitement of listening to, as well as creating, music along with really writing something for too many years now. I have felt guilty for years now. I feel guilty beyond words about these things. For example, when [we] were backstage and the lights go out and the manic roar of the crowd begins, it doesn't affect me in the way it did for Freddie Mercury who seemed to relish and love the adoration of the crowd. That is something I admire and envy. The fact is that I can't fool you. Any one of you. It simply isn't fair to you or me. The worst crime I can think of would be to put people off by faking it and pretending I'm having 100% fun. Sometimes I feel as if I should have to punch a clock before I walk out on stage. I've tried everything in my power to appreciate it and I do. God believe me I do – but it's not enough."

Cobain talked about the unwanted success he had achieved with his band, the unhappiness it had brought, and the more desperate thoughts that had driven him over the edge: "I hate it, I can't play with them any more, it's not fun for me any more, I can't live this life. I appreciate the fact that we have affected and entertained a lot of people. I must be one of those narcissists who only enjoys things when they're alone. I'm too sensitive. I have to be slightly numb to regain the enthusiasm I once had as a child. There is good in all of us and I simply love people too much. So much so that it makes me feel too sad… sad little sensitive unappreciated Pisces Jesus Man. And I had it good, very good, I'm grateful. But since the age of seven I've become hateful towards all humans in general, only because I love and feel for people too much I guess. I thank you all from the bottom of my burning nauseous stomach for your letters and concern during the last years. I'm too much of an erratic, moody person. I don't have the passion any more. It's better to burn out than to fade away."

As a shocked music world tried to piece together the timetable of events surrounding Kurt's death, it soon became clear that the Cobains' lifestyle was volatile in the extreme.

There were several irregularities in the exact sequence of events. Knowledge of Cobain's most recent whereabouts seemed no more than sketchy. On the weekend before his body was discovered he admitted himself into a drug rehabilitation clinic in Hollywood to undergo intervention therapy, whereby an addict is confronted by friends and family about their prob-

lem. After two days of this, Cobain had reacted angrily to the band members in one such session and had "gone over the wire" – quite literally escaping by jumping over the fence of the clinic. He failed to get in touch with Courtney, which was unusual.

His concerned mother filed a missing persons report, telling local reporters she was scared for her son's safety. "He is probably going to turn up dead and join that stupid club I told him not to join," she said, referring to the cortège of rock stars who'd taken their own lives. The missing report suggested Kurt "had bought a shotgun and may be suicidal".

Meanwhile it is alleged Love hired a team of private investigators to track down her husband, but to no avail. By Wednesday concern was growing and Seattle police informed workers at the family home to report immediately if he was sighted. Unconfirmed reports suggested a 911 emergency call had been made regarding an incident the day before the body was found but a second call claimed the first was a hoax.

Police claimed to have made periodic visits to the house over the course of the final week and uncovered nothing. "It was something I felt was not unusual that he would disappear like that," stated a senior officer. "I thought he may not have been a truly missing person, but a person who didn't want to be found." The only confirmed sightings of Kurt during the previous week came from neighbours who had seen him walking in a nearby park, looking thin and unwell, and wrapped in a heavy topcoat despite the warm weather. The mystery deepened when it became known that Cobain might have spent a night with an unknown friend at another house he owned. Fresh tyre tracks

were found outside this house, and inside there was a sleeping bag which didn't belong to Cobain, and an ashtray full of cigarette butts not usually smoked by Cobain, stubbed out next to the singer's usual brand.

Courtney Love's whereabouts were no less mysterious. She had been in LA, along with baby Frances Bean, to promote her forthcoming album with her band Hole, ironically entitled 'Live Through This', and also to undergo psychiatric treatment for emotional and drug reliance problems.

On April 4 she cancelled the first date of a UK tour in order to "focus on the greater good – the health and happiness of her immediate family" according to her management.

On April 7, the day before Cobain's body was found, she phoned the front desk of her hotel and asked for a doctor as she had suffered an allergic reaction to a prescribed drug. She was rushed to hospital, and later released, at which point she was immediately arrested for possession of a controlled substance, drug paraphernalia and stolen property, charges furiously denied by her lawyer, as were claims that she had actually overdosed on heroin in the hotel room. In the room police allegedly found a bag of white powder (claimed by her lawyer to be 'a Buddhist luck potion'), a hypodermic needle, and a prescription pad used by doctors to obtain drugs. She was released on $10,000 bail.

The whereabouts of her eighteen-month-old baby were also unclear at this stage, although she later turned up at the Love's family home. Indications of Love's troubled life were suspected by Robert Hilburn of the *LA Times* who interviewed her on the Monday and suspected family trouble. The interview was never published as it was overcome by events, but Hilburn later claimed she looked fragile and frightened and burst into tears when talking about Cobain, insisting on talking off the record as she described the tensions in their relationship. She also admitted to Hilburn that she had a serious drug problem. "I accepted the fact I was a drug addict and I go to meetings (of Narcotics Anonymous). I am aware I am not above it, I realise drugs can floor me." She was evidently unaware that 1,000 miles away, her husband lay dead on the floor of their home.

Taking the bizarre and tragic events back further, it is clear that the Cobain family had been struggling for some time to come to terms with the excessive media attention, drug use and instability caused by their rigorous careers. On March 18, Love had called the emergency services after Cobain locked himself in his room with three guns and said he wanted to kill himself. When the police arrived he told them he just wanted to stay away from his wife for a while and was not suicidal. The police

'HE WOULD HAVE LEFT THIS WORLD SEVERAL YEARS AGO IF HE HADN'T MET COURTNEY' DANNY GOLDBURG, MANAGER

'I'VE BECOME HATEFUL TOWARDS ALL HUMANS IN GENERAL, ONLY BECAUSE I LOVE AND FEEL FOR PEOPLE TOO MUCH' *KURT*

'I THINK OF MY NEW SONGS AS POP SONGS... THAT'S JUST TOO BORING, I'D RATHER HAVE A GOOD HOOK' *KURT*

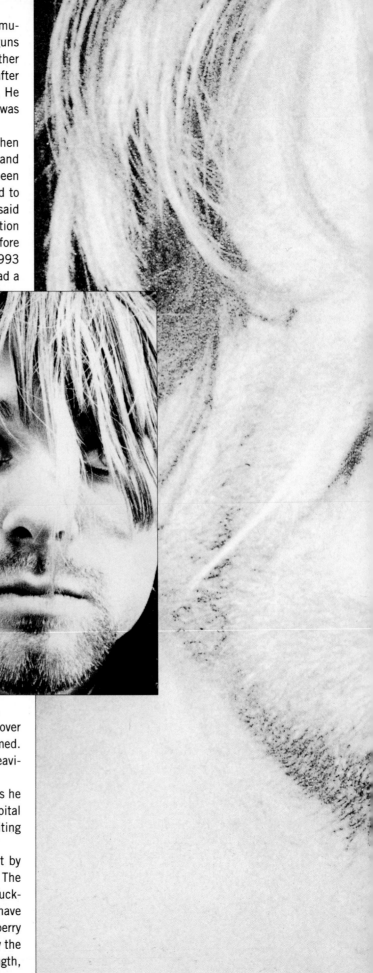

took no chances, and confiscated the arms, 25 boxes of ammunition and a number of bottles of unidentified pills. These guns had also been taken from Cobain in June of 1993 after another argument which saw Love throw fruit juice in his face, after which she claimed he pushed her then tried to choke her. He was arrested and taken to the jail for three hours but there was not enough evidence to press charges.

A month earlier, Love claimed to have helped Cobain when he had overdosed. He'd arrived back from a party delirious and passed out, having injected $40 worth of heroin. Love had been forced to inject him with buprenophine, a substance used to kickstart people's bodies when they have overdosed. She said he was suffering from cotton fever, an excruciating condition whereby fibre from cotton wool used to filter the heroin before use accidentally gets into the blood stream. In May of 1993 Love claimed this had happened before. Clearly Cobain had a history of drug problems. The most public indication that something was seriously wrong came on March 4 1994 with the news that Cobain had gone into a critical drug and alcohol induced coma in Rome. Earlier Nirvana had played a weak, 40-minute show at the Giaccio Ice Rink in Marino, during which Kurt had not said a single word to his audience. From there they had travelled to Germany for a further two concerts, but Cobain cancelled both, complaining of a sore throat. Back in Italy, Courtney Love had awoken in the early hours and had been unable to wake Kurt when she saw blood trickling from his nose. By 7am and under the false name of Kurt Poupon, he was in a critical condition in the local hospital; by midday of March 4 the news was spreading that he had gone into an irreversible coma. In their hotel room police allegedly found champagne, and a bottle of Roipnol, a tranquilliser popular among Italian drug addicts.

It later became apparent that Cobain had swallowed over sixty pills. Rumours of a suicide note were unconfirmed. Speculation heightened when he was moved to a private, heavily guarded clinic nearby.

Many feared he was in no condition to be moved unless he was beyond hope, and the media went into a frenzy. Hospital staff were briefed and ordered to say nothing to those waiting outside.

During the day he drifted in and out of the coma but by evening he had stirred, and was responding to his name. The first thing he wrote on a pad to the doctors was "Get these fucking tubes out of my nose".The first thing he is reported to have said was "fuck you", or alternatively "Can I have a strawberry milkshake" depending on which magazine you believe. By the Saturday he was sitting up in bed and regaining strength,

COBAIN EXPRESSED REPEATED RESERVATIONS ABOUT THE SINCERITY OF WHAT THEY WERE DOING

'SEATTLE WAS FAMOUS NOW FOR GRUNGE, CAPPUCCINO AND HEROIN' ***COURTNEY***

although he was unsure of what had happened to him as his memory was still hazy from the effects of drugs. Nirvana's management issued a transparent press release stating that he had suffered 'a complete collapse due to fatigue and severe influenza' whereafter complications arose after 'he had combined prescription pain killers and alcohol'. (This was a rather futile attempt to imply that Cobain was drug free. Recent after-show parties had apparently been devoid of any alcohol, a claim supported by Tony Barber of The Buzzcocks, who had appeared on Nirvana's European tour and noted how clean Cobain had lived, although he also noted how alone and lost he appeared.) By Monday Kurt was alert and tests showed that the higher centres of his brain were still intact, the loss of them could have led to what is classed as a 'persistent vegetative state'. He left the hospital on March 8, immediately going into hiding with his wife and child to recuperate. All was not well however – Love told the *LA Times* that "after Rome I just couldn't take it".

If the events before Kurt's death were complex, the immediate aftermath was equally as dramatic and rumour-ridden. Love was besieged by the media. She announced the family would be staying on at the house where Cobain killed himself, saying "I'm not leaving this house, this is the house Kurt wanted us to have". Her attitude towards him mellowed somewhat from the angry shouts of 'asshole' that had rung out across the vigil a week earlier, but she was distraught whenever she appeared on television. On one show she talked of Cobain's drug problems, and how he "was very depressed...some people just have thin skins". She urged Nirvana fans not to see drug use as glamorous or problem solving, and criticised the Seattle police for the easy availability of heroin in the city, saying Seattle was famous now for grunge, cappuccino and heroin. One of her public appearances ended with her desperately mumbling, "I'm tough and I can take anything, but I can't take this".

A toxicology report on Kurt's body stated that there was a high concentration of heroin in his body, up to twice the amount that can usually kill, as well as Valium and Diazepan,

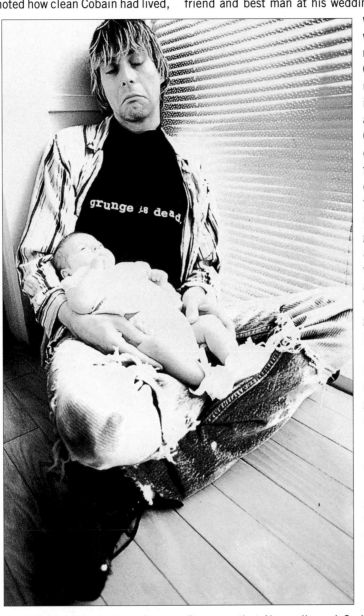

both tranquillisers. This raised the question that Cobain was probably intoxicated at the time of his actual death and might therefore have been unaware of what he was doing. Also, it transpired he had lain dead for three days, which cast confusion over the various claims by several parties that they had been searching 'frantically' for him.

It is unlikely that a high profile figure such as Cobain could be 'missing' for five days, only to eventually be found at his home. The gun was bought for him on April 2 by his long time friend and best man at his wedding, Dylan Carlson, guitarist with band Earth, before he went to LA for the drug rehabilitation programme. Carlson said he was unaware that the Rome incident was being treated as a suicide attempt. He felt Cobain had not appeared depressed or suicidal when they bought the gun, and claimed he wanted the gun for self-protection. One unconfirmed report suggested that Kurt called another of his friends the week before and inquired about the most efficient way to kill yourself with a gun. This also went unreported at the time.

Other rumours took a more personal, character-damaging turn. Some suggested Love had left Cobain and started an affair with Evan Dando of The Lemonheads, claims that were furiously denied by both parties. According to some sources, the marriage was in trouble, and there was conjecture that the social services were preparing to take custody of the couple's baby as they had been deemed unfit parents. Rumours that Novoselic and Grohl, exasperated by the lead singer's chronic drug and personal problems, had left Nirvana, remained unconfirmed, although when they dropped out of the Lollapalooza tour and cancelled their own dates there was clearly something wrong. The rumours were unlikely to decrease now that Cobain was dead – if anything, the incident merely fanned the flames of a hungry media, who had already drained the couple of story after story over recent months.

Until they had satiated their enormous appetite for unsubstantiated rumour, the fourth member of the Cobain family to commit suicide would never be able to rest in peace.

HE WAS THIS GENERATION'S MOST INSPIRATIONAL SONGWRITER

'FINALLY ONE NIGHT...KURT SAID TO ME
'YOU KNOW I'M NOT ALWAYS LIKE THIS'' DAVE GROHL

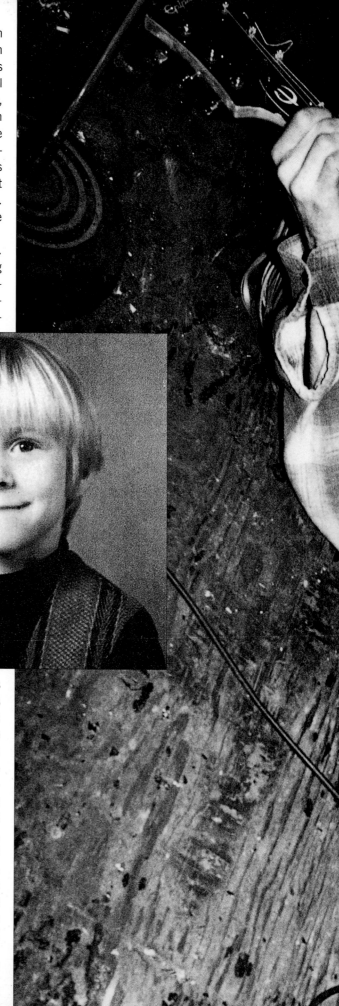

Kurt Cobain was born on February 20, 1967, in Aberdeen, an isolated US town one hundred miles from the Pacific Canadian border renowned only for its logging industry. As a youngster his diminutive frame stopped him from aspiring to either the local trade or other physically demanding areas of All American life, and he became a loner in the community, pursuing interests in art and culture, usually accompanied by an imaginary friend he called Boda. He was a sickly child, suffering from chronic bronchitis and a minor curvature of the spine; emotionally he was resolute and happy, despite his solitude, until the age of eight when his secretary mother and machinist father were divorced. For two years he lived with his father in a caravan trailer before returning to live with his mother at the original family home.

The effect of the divorce on the young boy was traumatic. Henceforth he carried with him a general mistrust of anything and everything, and he began to internalise his feelings, seeking solace in petty crimes. By all accounts he become something of a local weird case, flirting with homosexuality, breaking-and-entering and vandalism. During one spray frenzy he emblazoned the slogan "God is gay' around town, blasphemy which cost him a three day suspended sentence. He hated the alcoholic apathy of the community, the nauseating macho bravado of his school peers and the insular nature of Aberdeen, and he determined to break away from it all.

Kurt's interest in music was fuelled by both parents, although he particularly liked his Dad's Black Sabbath and Beatles records. In 1976 he was devastated to discover that The Fab Four would never come to play in his home town as they had broken up six years previously. Similarly, punk was also something he could only read about. The Sex Pistols inspired him but it wasn't until 1981 that the local music library stocked a copy of The Clash's 'Sandinista' LP, hardly the ideal introduction to punk rock. Cobain was not impressed with what he heard and began to look elsewhere for musical fulfilment. Local band The Melvins were the only touchable magazine heroes he could have and he followed them faithfully, even carrying gear and fixing drinks for them. Occasionally he played one of his own compositions to their guitarist Buzz Osbourne, with whom he became friendly. The Melvins never progressed commercially but at one time ruled the underground in Seattle, releasing enigmatic singles on the Alchemy label. Cobain's first sight of The Melvins on stage made quite an impact on his musically open mind. "When I saw them play they just blew me away," he said. "I was instantly a punk rocker. I abandoned all my friends and I got a spiky haircut."

The young Cobain also started listening to a wider variety of

'I WAS INSTANTLY A PUNK ROCKER. I ABANDONED ALL MY FRIENDS AND I GOT A SPIKY HAIRCUT' KURT

THE BEATLES FOR MELODIC STIMULUS

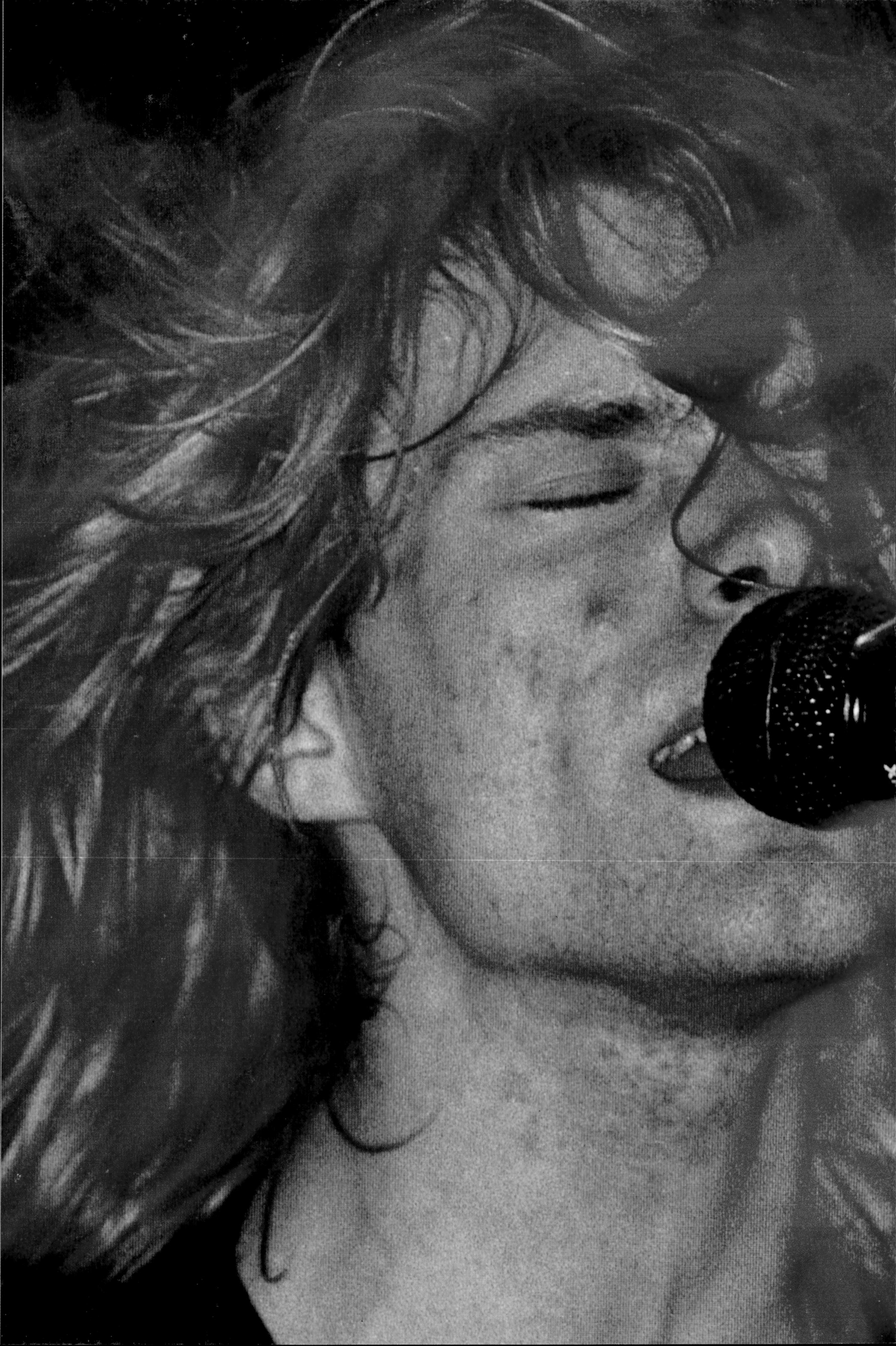

rock – The Wipers, Led Zeppelin, Kiss, Big Black and Black Flag (whom he thought were too macho but liked both Henry Rollins' vulnerability and the music), and he was also attracted to oddballs, feminists, outsiders like Young Marble Giants, The Raincoats, Jad Fair, acts whose music agreed with his sensibilities. His sense of being an outsider was compounded by the geography of punk in the US. Unlike in Britain, Cobain could walk for a thousand miles and not meet someone with similar tastes, such was the desolation of his town. Punk provided existential solace for a while but he soon began to look to forming his own band.

It was Buzz from The Melvins who introduced Kurt to a gangly local lad of Yugoslavian origin called Chris Novoselic, who seemed to share a similar sense of displacement to Cobain. He too dropped out of school, having been uprooted to Aberdeen from his native LA suburb. On arriving in Aberdeen he immediately realised no-one liked the same music as him – Led Zeppelin, Devo, Kiss – no-one that is, except Kurt Cobain. They formed their first band, Ed Ted and Fred, with a friend, but this was rapidly replaced by another line-up, after which several personnel and name changes followed in quick succession. At one show where they played as Skid Row, no-one turned up at all so they just packed up and went home. They were not to be deterred, however, and by 1985, under the moniker of Fecal Matter, Kurt and Chris had made a demo of songs that were vignettes of Aberdeen life, actually little more than character assassinations of local stereotypes.

Their progress over the next few years was rapid and considerable. Cobain now listened to straightedge hardcore bands like Minor Threat, whose very philosophical and intensely serious music revolted against the outrages of punk, in some songs even advocating against drugs and sex. Although musically appealing, this was never likely to attract the young Cobain's subversive streak and he looked to groups like Flipper and Scratch Acid for more inspiring music and lifestyles: punk, but anti-hardcore. Scratch Acid were renowned for their vocalist's tortured howls and screams and Cobain learnt from their singer David Yow how to treat his voice as an instrument. These bands contributed anarchic freedom to Cobain's developing musical vision, on top of which he continually looked back to The Beatles for melodic stimulus.

By 1986 all these various influences had congealed to create a music and vocal style that was highly original. In September 1986 19-year-old Kurt recorded another demo with Chris and drummer Dale Crover of The Melvins, which included songs called 'Spank Thru', 'Floyd The Barber' and 'Negative

'WE WOULD SIT IN THIS TINY SHOEBOX APARTMENT FOR EIGHT HOURS AT A TIME WITHOUT SAYING A WORD' *DAVE GROHL*

'IT'S NOT HARD TO KEEP YOUR DIGNITY AND SIGN TO A MAJOR LABEL' *KURT*

Creep'. Soon after he moved to Seattle and broke away from Aberdeen at last.

This was also the year that the seven-year-old Seattle based Sub Pop fanzine of local fame and influence graduated into a fully fledged record label, soon to begin its prestigious series of single releases on limited edition coloured vinyl, the first of which was the compilation album 'Sub Pop 100' in 1986. Sub Pop, partnered by Bruce Pavitt and Jonathan Poneman, championed Seattle's local underground, which was healthy and innovative in the early Eighties, with bands like Mother Love Bone (later splintering into Pearl Jam), Malfunkshen and Green River. Even during 1983, when the lack of commercial success crushed much of the life out of the scene, Sub Pop continued to fight their corner. Competing against the enormous commercial success of local bands like Queensrÿche, the label would ultimately introduce America to a roster of great bands.

Soundgarden were the first to transpose their local following on to a national scale. Mudhoney and Tad followed, and in 1987 the label signed Cobain's band, now called Nirvana, on the basis of a demo tape he had recorded the previous autumn, and a meeting in a downtown coffee shop. It was the first band the label had signed on the strength of a demo, and Sub Pop had high hopes for them.

At this stage Nirvana was unable to find a regular drummer, a problem that would plague them until 1990 when Dave Grohl finally filled the spot permanently. Signing to Sub Pop was a wise move: their timing was good, as this year saw an increased level of awareness about the underground scene, inspired by the ability of bands like Sonic Youth to reach wider audiences. With the label's money Cobain, Novoselic and Dale Crover cut their first single,

'Love Buzz' (a cover of an original by Dutch pop band Shocking Blue), at Jack Endino's studio where Sub Pop bands often recorded. Ironically it was a love song, far removed from the angry style of diatribe for which Cobain would later become renowned. The response to the single was good, and the 1,000 copies were sold, but Nirvana still palled in comparison to others on the label, especially Tad and Mudhoney. The former took their out-sized frontman across Europe and received wild applause, whilst the 1988 début by Mudhoney, the LP 'Superfuzz Bigmuff', left them with the punk world at their feet.

Meanwhile Nirvana went into the studio in June 1989 for a three day recording session (costing just $606.17) which gave birth to 'Bleach'. Featuring new drummer Chad Channing, this was the first opportunity to see Cobain's developing writing skills at length. The response to the album suggested Sub

Pop's unusually intense faith had been well-placed – it was an absurdly belligerent LP, dealing with small town America, the battle of the sexes, Cobain's love for punk, and – on 'Negative Creep' – paedophilia, though the message of the songs was lost because the vocals were too low in the mix. Nevertheless, it was a vital and impressive statement, lashed with the flavour of Sonic Youth and compared by some to a cross between The Pixies and Soul Asylum. Recording quickly resulted in a sparse, barren production which gave the project an invigorating sense of urgency, with basic drum patterns thrashing through with the heavy, repeated riffing that was to become Nirvana's trademark. It was mostly hard rock, but there were pop moments too, notably 'About A Girl' and 'Sifting'. The album sold well, and in Britain DJ John Peel plugged it on his cult show and in the broadsheet *Observer* newspaper, while the weekly music press also responded warmly. Even so, the caricatured North Western lifestyle Mudhoney portrayed was still winning the best reviews and Nirvana were still very much the Seattle underdogs.

Prior to the 'Bleach' sessions, the band had taken on Jason Everman on second guitar, but he was reluctant to tour, and although his face appears on 'Bleach', he did not contribute to it and left soon after. That autumn, the three piece supported Tad around the UK for between £50 and £100 per gig, and in December they opened the Sub Pop Lamefest bill at London's Astoria, a similar affair to a Seattle show in June, where Nirvana blew Mudhoney and Tad offstage with a blistering set, followed by the auto-destruct fest that was becoming a staple part of their live show. The British press suddenly wanted to know who they were and where they had come from – the focus of attention was shifting.

Nirvana now began to garner interest from the major labels, and Sub Pop knew they needed major distribution if they were to keep their best bands. A proposed deal with CBS fell through at the very last minute, though Nirvana was the prime bait to tempt the major label to sign on the dotted line. So 1990 was something of a static year for the ascending Nirvana, with a UK tour cancelled in March after they lost their fourth drummer Chad Channing just before flying out. This latest personnel change could not have come at a worse time – interest in the band was high and gigs would have galvanised this interest and raised the stakes for inquiring majors. Instead they spent the next six months trying to find a replacement, and the music press was filled with rumours of who that would be.

At one point J Mascis of Dinosaur Jr thought about leaving that band and resuming his original instrument for Nirvana, while other recruits included the return of Dale Crover from The

SPARSE, BARREN PRODUCTION WHICH GAVE THE PROJECT AN INVIGORATING SENSE OF URGENCY

Melvins or Dan Peters from Mudhoney, who actually played on the sessions for the 'Sliver' single released on Sub Pop in the summer of 1990. It was not until October that Crover suggested they phone Dave Grohl from highly respected Washington band The Scream (formerly of less well respected Dain Bramage). He auditioned and was immediately accepted. Grohl moved into Cobain's flat where he was surprised by the singer's moods. "We would sit in this tiny shoebox apartment for eight hours at a time without saying a word. For weeks and weeks this happened. Finally one night we were driving back in the van and Kurt said to me 'You know I'm not always like this'."

Stable at last, Nirvana were able to actively pursue the major label offers they had been receiving, and by the New Year they had decided on Geffen, thus cutting out Sub Pop. A $250,000 deal was signed, with the band's original label getting a healthy pay-off. Although at the time some narrow-minded purists criticised Nirvana's principles for signing to a major label, Cobain had no such qualms. "It's not hard to keep your dignity and sign to a major label," he said. "Most people don't even have the dignity in the first place." One key reason for signing to a major was to enable young kids to have access to his music and not come up against the limitations he had with so many of his favourite bands in his own youth. His ideal was to follow the example of Sonic Youth, a band to whom he would constantly refer as a yardstick for his own group's integrity.

At the end of 1990 Cobain gave a small clue as to where Nirvana's music was heading on the new label. "As time goes on, my songs are getting poppier and poppier as I get happier and happier. The songs are now about conflicts in relationships, emotional things with other human beings. Pop is something we've always been aware of and are just now starting to express. I think of my new songs as pop songs, there won't be any songs as heavy as 'Bleach' on the new record. That's just too boring, I'd rather have a good hook." Not even Nirvana's most charitable reviewers could have imagined the impact that this slight change in musical emphasis would have over the next eighteen months.

With Butch Vig at the controls, and Andy Wallace (of Slayer fame) mixing, Nirvana began work on their second album at Sound City Studios in Van Nuys, California. That same week America bombed Baghdad in response to Iraq's invasion of Kuwait, thus triggering off the Gulf War. With a budget of $100,000, relatively low for Geffen, they were confident that the original 40,000 pressing would sell out and a hundred thousand or more might sell over a period of time. Recording was dominated by speedy but precise work, and a mixture of

Jack Daniels and hypodermic cough syrup. The album was released in September 1991, before which Nirvana hit the road again, inciting frenzied reactions in every city they played. But this was nothing compared to the blitzkrieg of attention that would soon come their way.

The album itself was a barrage of grunge anthems (an unnecessary generic term coined by Poneman of Sub Pop) that showed Cobain's pop sensibilities at their peak. His heavy repetitive riffing played over the thunderous bass and drums toyed with Beatles-ish melodies one minute and the enraged screams of a man at the end of his tether the next. John Lennon would have been proud of Kurt. The dynamics of the album were astonishing, switching from sensitive, sparse interludes to all-out, violent aural assaults. The punk monster 'Territorial Pissings' was balanced beautifully against slower moments like 'Come As You Are'. As one reviewer remarked, this was "pop fronted by a serial killer". Lyrically obtuse at times, there were two direct thematical pieces, most disturbingly the story of a brutal rape told from the imbalanced mind of the perpetrator, and 'Something In The Way' which explained Cobain's alienation from his home town. The vocal delivery was fragmentary, evocative, deep and it worked. 'Nevermind' was a juggernaut of a record.

Geffen's faith appeared to have been as well placed as Sub Pop's original belief, but not even the most arrogant of major label scouts could have predicted what would happen next. Over the following twelve months, the world was gripped by a band which stood for everything that the corporate music industry opposed. First indications of the incredible reaction came with the response to the single 'Smells Like Teen Spirit', named after a teenage deodorant Cobain had spotted in a drug store. Alternative radio stations played the single constantly, then MTV latched on to the video for the record, which although disliked by Cobain triggered off an immense empathy among viewers. After an initial showing on the alternative programme *120 Minutes* the response was so strong that the video was switched to the mainstream shows, and soon notched up to ten plays per day, guaranteeing Nirvana huge coverage among the millions of kids who treated MTV as a virtual religion.

The band thus opened the door to the colossal mainstream market, previously shut to their contemporaries, and within months they had conquered it. The accolades and landmark sales came flooding in: by December 70,000 people were walking into a record shop and buying 'Nevermind' every day – that's 150 people a minute. The same month 'Teen Spirit' rose to MTV's No.1 video spot. In the first six weeks the album sold one million copies; by January that figure had reached four million and in the process knocked Michael Jackson's 'Dangerous' album off the American No.1 spot. Nirvana appeared on *Saturday Night Live* (on which Cobain and Novoselic French-kissed) and every front cover, including *Rolling Stone* magazine. Every show sold out in a matter of minutes, and even Axl Rose wanted backstage passes for their shows (and was duly refused). Back copies of 'Bleach' also started to fly off the shelves.

With 'Nevermind' at No.1, Britain too was gripped by 'Nirvanamania' as every mainstream tabloid and glossy magazine now wanted a piece of a band who were virtually unknown only six months ago. At the grass roots level, the impact was perhaps even more startling – the record was being bought by an unprecedented cross-over of fans. Metal heads latched onto the heavy riffing whilst pop kids put off thrash metal's lack of melody opted for Cobain's distinctive hooks. Disillusioned rock fans swarmed to Nirvana's side, and many women were attracted by their non-macho stance, the lack of masturbatory pretence and sexist innuendoes, and the all-male atmosphere that had so tediously dominated this area of music for years. In short, the album traversed many musical barriers and eliminated the genre snobbery that pervaded the marketplace.

It was no surprise that within a matter of weeks Nirvana had lost all sense of perspective and control over their careers. This was one of the most rapid escalations to supremacy the music world had seen for years. "We thought we'd sell a couple hundred thousand records at the most and that would be fine," said Chris Novoselic. "Next thing you know we go Top 10". Eventually their 'alternative' record would go on to sell over 10 million copies worldwide, grossing $40 million in the process, leaving Nirvana on top of a pop world against which they had once so defiantly rebelled.

The amazing commercial success of 'Nevermind' was irrefutable – what was less clear was why it had such an effect. There were two schools of thought. The first was that the record itself was simply a masterpiece with universal appeal that was compelling to an enormous audience. The second acknowledges the validity of the record but suggests that it was also a case of Nirvana being in the right place at the right time. The huge metal market had become bloated with soft-porn videos and self-indulgent, endless solo axe heroes, while the pure underground couldn't break free of its cult origins. In addition, the present social environment left much of American youth disenfranchised, dissatisfied and in need of inspiration. 'Teen Spirit' captured that essence, that feeling of belonging outside

the mainstream, and 'Nevermind' continued that association across an entire album, seizing the ideas and emotions of a frustrated generation strangled by uncaring politicians and a cultural wasteland.

Not that the band had any time to sit back and consider these lofty assertions. The phenomenal success of the album was reinforced by a massive world tour, taking them through America, Europe, Britain, Japan and Australasia, which confirmed the worldwide nature of their appeal. The shows at this point were chaotic, inspirational affairs: venues packed to bursting, PA's loud enough to explode and the band in full noise violence mode. More than anything the singer's aggressive voice captured the fans' psyche and passion – Cobain's open throated haemorrhages on stage were even more tortured and caustic than on record, whilst his two companions clubbed their instruments into submission, and with them the crowd as well. The shows on this tour had an over-riding sense of the perverse and berserk, the rage and resignation mixing to dramatic effect. The frustrations of being on the road so long began to take their toll on the instruments – the bill for smashed gear went way beyond their $750 a week allowance.

Under such huge media focus and rigorous schedules, it was perhaps inevitable that cracks would show, and unfortunately the cracks that did appear were serious. The same month that 'Nirvanamania' swept the world, Cobain started using heroin. He shared his habit with his new-found girlfriend, Courtney Love, lead singer with the excellent Hole, whom in December 1991 he had declared was "the best fuck in the world". The daughter of Grateful Dead roadie Hank Harrison, she had allegedly attended Woodstock aged three and dropped acid before she even went to school. In the mid-Seventies she went to Australia where she earned a living as a stripper, before moving on to Liverpool in 1982. Returning to America in 1984, she formed her first band Sugar Baby Doll, shared an apartment with Lydia Lunch and played a punk cameo role in the film *Sid And Nancy*. Cobain was strongly attracted by her individuality and feminist stance, and chased her around the European tour circuit in late 1991. Her arrival on the Nirvana scene marked the start of a real life soap opera.

Simultaneously, the success of 'Nevermind' threw the band into a tailspin, with Novoselic acquiring a drink problem and Grohl a reputation for carnal excess. Meanwhile a dramatic sub-plot was developing that would eventually overwhelm the music that had made the band so popular in the first place. A handful of shows had to be cancelled due to a 'sore throat' and rumours started to circulate about the general health of the

'I DON'T THINK COURTNEY AND I ARE THAT FUCKED UP.
...WE HAVE JUST LACKED LOVE ALL OUR LIVES' ***KURT***

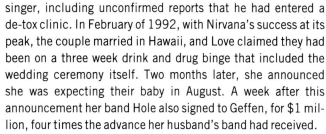

singer, including unconfirmed reports that he had entered a de-tox clinic. In February of 1992, with Nirvana's success at its peak, the couple married in Hawaii, and Love claimed they had been on a three week drink and drug binge that included the wedding ceremony itself. Two months later, she announced she was expecting their baby in August. A week after this announcement her band Hole also signed to Geffen, for $1 million, four times the advance her husband's band had received.

The media now had a rock and roll couple to report on and they set about their task in earnest. One interview quoted Love as saying she was smoking while pregnant because she wanted a small baby. Heroin abuse rumours were common-place, claims fuelled when Cobain was rushed to hospital after collapsing with "a stomach ulcer" after a show at Belfast Kings Hall, which his management blamed on "junk food and vocal technique". The media did not stop at mere ill health. In June Cobain was reported to have died in a car crash. A ban on press relations in April did not deter the press. Stories began to filter through that Cobain and Love had become isolated from Novoselic and Grohl, and that Cobain was hen-pecked. She had apparently refused to let Chris' wife attend the wedding and told Cobain to avoid certain journalists she disliked. Deliberately or not, Love exacerbated the situation with her provocative quotes, and she was soon portrayed as an evil, scheming witch, clawing at her husband's independence and spirit. Her maternal skills were brought into question by the media in July when she was reported to have been admitted to hospital with a damaged womb; one magazine even claimed she was racing around on motorbikes weeks before she was due to give birth.

Meanwhile, the band released a compilation album of B-sides and out-takes called 'Incesticide' that sold massively.

Sensationalist stories had begun to compete with the band's commercial success, but in July they completely overshadowed it when *Vanity Fair* ran an article claiming that Love had knowingly used heroin while five months pregnant, a claim that provoked a furious and absolute denial from the couple. Comparing them to Sid Vicious and Nancy Spungen, the piece generally attacked their ethical fibre, and observers began to take sides.

Most saw Cobain as the weaker of the two, under Love's influence, which was strange since only weeks before the same commentators had hailed him as the spokesman for a generation. For their part, the couple defended themselves as best they could, with Cobain regularly repeating his statements of new-found happiness.

Cobain was devastated by some of the allegations and at one

'IF I'M GOING TO TAKE DRUGS THAT'S MY OWN FUCKING PREROGATIVE, IT'S NOBODY'S BUSINESS' KURT stage it was rumoured that they had contemplated a joint sui-cide. He claimed she had totally changed him when he said, "I'm not as much of a neurotic, unstable person as I was. I used to feel I was always alone, even though I had a lot of friends and a band." He also said, "Courtney certainly helped me put Nirvana in perspective, to realise that my reality doesn't entire-ly revolve around the band, that I can deal without it if I have to." In response to the drug rumours and unstable jibes he said, "I don't think Courtney and I are that fucked up. We have just lacked love all our lives."

Once the crushing world tour for 'Nevermind' was complete the band could finally rest and pause for breath. Their monu-mental headline performance at Reading had refuted the wide-spread rumours of a Nirvana split, although they had very nearly imploded with their own success. Despite the birth of a healthy baby girl, Frances Bean Cobain, in August, and Cobain's claims that this new arrival had changed his life for the better, the rumour mill did not stop. Headlines ran that it was a junkie baby and that Love had been using heroin up to two weeks before the birth, all uncon-firmed and highly question-able. An old Irish band received an out of court settle-ment, claiming they had been using the name Nirvana for years. A doctor was threatened with legal action by Love after he revealed details of alleged treatment for drug use. In October news broke of an unof-ficial and highly damaging Nirvana biography by two fans-turned authors, and the famous couple's reactions raised the stakes. Cobain left abusive and threatening mes-sages on the authors' answer phone while Love allegedly assaulted one of the writers at a club in Hollywood.

The couple had already fallen victim to the long acknow-ledged fact that rock and roll is more interesting, and therefore more sellable, when there is scandal and controversy. Cobain the millionaire drugged-up rock star married to a peroxide Nancy Spungen double who was even more volatile was the stuff of which headlines are made, and most journalists pur-sued this mythology whether it was actually true or not. With a Hollywood 'grunge' film starring Matt Dillon and Bridget Fonda on release, and designers like Mark Jacobs and Christian Roth exhibiting their 'grunge' collections, one fact was unquestion-able – the underground was dead, and for many Seattle had moved from a Mecca to a cliché in six months.

Against this turbulent back-drop the band recorded their third album, a difficult and unenviable task, and progress was not helped when Cobain's lyric book was destroyed in a flood at the house. Their aim was to reduce all the clumsy deliberation usually associated with major bands, to kick against the pre-conceptions that now surrounded them. Steve Albini of Big Black fame produced the record at Pachyderm Recording Studios in Minnesota, and the majority of the tracks were (again) recorded in an astonishing three day session, which Cobain said was one of the most richly productive of his career – over 80% of the vocals for the album were recorded in one day alone. The working title of the album was 'I Hate Myself And I Want To Die', a chillingly prophetic choice, but one that Cobain belittled as tongue-in-cheek. Before, during, and after the recording, the band was the subject of as many rumours as they had suffered in their private lives. Albini was falling out with them, or with Geffen; Geffen had refused to release the record because it was so violently against what they had expected; Nirvana's management were worried that the record would be so barren and harsh as to be inaccessible. All these rumours and more flew around and only served to heighten anticipation before release. It was finally titled 'In Utero', meaning 'back to the womb'. The album was much darker than its predecessor and delved deep into the psy-che of Cobain's troubled mind and desperate thoughts.

The benefit of hindsight prejudices lyrical analysis but several lines are worth the price of admission. The open-ing line is "Teenage angst has paid off well, now I'm bored and old" while on 'Milk It' Cobain appears to air his dark-est ideas, singing "I am my own pet virus, I don't need a host to live, We can feed off each other, we can share our endorphins". The chorus of this song includes his most frightening lyric yet: "Look on the bright side is suicide". Another song said "Use once and destroy" while his guilt ridden personality surfaces frequently with lines such as "What is wrong with me", "I'm so tired I can't sleep, I am a liar and a thief" and finally "All apologies, everything is my fault".

The thematical style seemed cathartic and highly personal, with manic results. Musically, the record was equally barren, though not as much as originally supposed. The drums and bass were sparse and thumping while Cobain's rasping vocal reached new heights of spitting fury on 'Milk It'. Cobain attacked the industry that had made him a rich man on tracks like 'Radio Friendly Unit Shifter', and other tracks' heavily con-fessional style was pervaded by a deep sense of guilt and frus-tration at his situation, as well as his confusion about the vio-lence of love. In many ways the record was a product of the environment the band's success had created, a self-drama reflecting their sudden notoriety and fame. 'In Utero' occupied a middle ground between Nirvana's other two records (although the songwriting was more sophisticated), and challenged the new legions of Nirvana fans to continue to like them after this grunge is dead.

more demanding release. It was a deliberate puncturing of the pop godhead crown he had acquired with 'Nevermind', a title he had not sought in the first place and from which he now clearly wanted to abdicate.

On release in September 1993, the record was generally acknowledged as a valid follow-up to the now multi-million 'Nevermind' and the band appeared to have beaten the curse of a major success choking future creativity. Some felt it was a confused record by a man unsure of his place in the new family and financial contentment he had found. Others thought its debauched and venomous vitriol showed the true side of Cobain's dark personality, a document of a mind in turmoil, in flux, dithering and dissatisfied.

The songs from 'In Utero' were previewed at the New York Music Seminar in July, Nirvana's first live show in The Big Apple since 1991. For this show they used Big John Duncan, the former Exploited guitarist and current Goodbye Mr MacKenzie man, to bolster their sound. To the amazement of on-lookers, they brought on cellos and acoustic guitars for the finale, which in true antag- onistic Nirvana style went down very badly. If nothing else this performance was proof that they could still con- found even their most faithful followers. At the same semi- nar, noisebangers Unsane lost their drummer Charlie Ondras to heroin, and the following week Stefan Sargent of Seattle's Seven Year Bitch died the same way.

The now bespectacled Cobain prepared himself for a gruelling world tour to promote the album, despite having requested a shorter schedule so he could spend time with his family. Pat Smears joined the band on guitar for the tour, their first in America since the autumn of 1991.

The shows were shockingly smooth and needless, to say, sold out instantly. Supported on some dates by The Buzzcocks, Nirvana appeared to have put all the speculation and rumour behind them, gelling again as a working unit and putting their music before everything else. Even 'Teen Spirit', at one stage dropped from the set from boredom, was played with a menac- ing relish.

As 1993 turned into 1994 though, it became clear that all was not well. Despite the growing catalogue of excellent reviews, rumours of Cobain's ill health returned, as did stories of disillusionment within Nirvana's ranks and Courtney's ques- tionable behaviour. The media and the music industry, as well as the record buying public, were by now used to such tales, and many turned a blind eye to the many scandals emanating from the Seattle base of the world's biggest alternative band. But nobody was ready for the news that broke on April 8.

Why did Cobain decide he no longer wanted to live? He had money, a beautiful young daughter, a wife with whom he was madly in love, and a band who were respected the world over as pioneering and even iconoclastic. Unfortunately, Cobain did not feel this was enough.

Several factors precipitated his demise. Firstly, his person- ality had always been volatile and prone to extreme mood swings and dark thoughts. This was exacerbated by spinal and stomach ailments which made touring painful and everyday life uncomfortable. Of the stomach pain he once said, "For five years during my stomach problem I wanted to kill myself every day. I came very close many times. It got to the point where I was on tour, lying on the floor, vomiting air because I couldn't hold down water. And I had to play a show in 20 minutes. I'd sing and cough up blood. This is no way to live a life. I love to play music but something was not right."

He initially sought medical help, but increasingly resorted to the pain killing effects of heroin to numb the pain.

Cobain carried with him a guilt complex from his par- ents' divorce, for which he blamed himself up until his early adult life, and which was worsened by his difficulty in coming to terms with his band's success. His feelings of alienation were at odds with his status as one of the world's leading songwriters, and this never rested well with him. His self-respect was in doubt, and his preference for the more feminine side of his character constantly clashed with the male dominated genre he led. He was genuinely and bitterly appalled when he heard that a young girl had been beaten and raped whilst her attackers played 'Polly' on a stereo. His non-macho ascension to the summit of a traditionally male-led rock market was one of his greatest achievements but it took its toll on his perplexed mind. In short, he was emotionally vulnerable, and his soul began to hurt as much as his stomach, hardly an ideal state for a man upon whom the lenses of the world's press were directly focused.

A second major reason for Cobain's malaise was his dissatis- faction with his celebrity status and the role of his band in an industry he still despised. As the hotels got bigger and intimate venues now meant 3,500 seaters, Cobain expressed repeated reservations about the sincerity of what they were doing. He no longer enjoyed playing before his audiences. In the press he complained that heavy metal fans – whom he disliked – enjoyed his music, but his gripes were unrealistic. His band was now public property and while he was entitled to be selective cre- atively he could hardly expect to limit whomsoever listened to his work. He also complained about being unable to go out in

'I'M DISGUSTED WITH HAVING TO DEAL WITH THE COMMERCIAL SIDE OF OUR BAND...' *KURT*

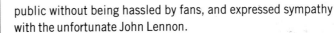
public without being hassled by fans, and expressed sympathy with the unfortunate John Lennon.

Many saw this as typical rock star whinging and little sympathy was forthcoming. "I'm disgusted with having to deal with the commercial side of our band at the moment and as a reaction I'm becoming more uptight and complain more," he stated. "It feels like I'm adopting a rock star attitude. I'm not pleasant to be around in those situations and I'm concerned that my band mates might be having a bad time. I had no idea that mainstream audiences react towards mainstream rock stars in this manner, because I've never paid attention to it before. I don't mean to complain as much as I do but it's a load of shit. It's really stupid. I've had days when I've considered this to be a job and I never thought that would happen. It makes me question the point of it all. I'm only going to bitch about it for another year and if I can't handle it after that, we're gonna have to make some pretty drastic changes."

Nevertheless, in early 1994 he announced that he was, in fact, a very happy person. "I still see stuff in magazines about Cobain, the whiny, neurotic, complaining, bitchy guy who hates everything, hates his life. I've never been happier in my life. I'm a much happier guy than a lot of people think I am." He also claimed he had beaten his heroin problem and that his family life was utterly stable.

This was not always the case, if at all. He dyed his hair purple as an act of rebellion when 'Nevermind' hit the charts. He talked of trying to go back to playing small clubs and hinted that his music might become more and more unpalatable to the commercial market. He clashed with his record company over the release dates of the third album and became embroiled in arguments with producer Steve Albini. He hated the enormous rounds of promotional appearances and the endless interviews. He gradually began to shrink away from the public eye which served only to heighten the value of a Cobain story by making it a scarcity. He failed to overcome his deep mistrust of the music business; he was appalled when 'Teen Spirit' was used to advertise antique cars.

This dissatisfaction affected his spirit at all levels, but especially on stage, where towards the end he often appeared static and communicated very little with the crowd. Of his decreasing enthusiasm for live shows he said, "I try every night, but I just can't fool myself. I'm not going to smile and pose like Eddie Van Halen." He was sick of the media exposure and scandal around him and his family, justified or not. "I have to hear rumours about me all the time, I'm totally fucking sick of it. If I'm going to take drugs that's my own fucking prerogative, it's nobody's business."

Since 'Nevermind' the music had been overshadowed by their lifestyles and careers, and the blinding spotlight Cobain found himself under as the vocalist ate away at his self-esteem. The titanic pressures and responsibilities of fame wore him down. The result – the irony – was that by becoming reclusive, he became the antithesis of what Nirvana once stood for. In many ways Cobain suffered from a classic Catch 22, that fame is the ultimate punk betrayal, that great acclaim is the antithesis of the music that put him there in the first instance, that anti-establishment behaviour might bring down one establishment but create another.

The third factor to exacerbate Cobain's unrest was his family. At the time of Frances Bean's birth he acknowledged the effect she had had on him. "Now I have this huge responsibility to my family and it's probably more pressure than I've ever had dealing with this band. I've started to evolve a little bit from being a completely negative bastard, pretending to be punk rock and hating the world, saying clichéd things." He doted on his daughter, taking her to concerts and award ceremonies, talking about the joys of fatherhood to anyone who would listen. His wife Love also seemed happy with married life, at least in public. Rumours of marriage problems, affairs and separations were all unsubstantiated. What was perhaps more worrying was the unconfirmed story that social services were considering custody of the baby and Cobain could not face the loss of his child. Ironic then, that if this is the case, his actions have lost her a father.

The final factor to disillusion Cobain was the limitation he felt Nirvana had imposed on him musically, a worry that he made entirely public. At one point in late 1993 he said, "I'm getting so tired of that formula, and it is a formula. We've mastered that for our band. We're all growing pretty tired of it. It is a dynamic style but there are a lot more things I could be using. We've been working on this formula for so long that it's literally becoming boring for us. We like playing that stuff but I don't know how much longer I can scream at the top of my lungs every night for an entire year on tour.

"We're almost exhausted. We've gone to the point where things are becoming repetitive, there's not something you can move up toward, there's not something you can look forward to. The best times that we ever had was when 'Nevermind' was coming out and we went on the American tour where we were playing clubs."

This frustration with the band's musical future did not have a crystal solution – he could not envisage a solo project but had spoken of several collaborations, including one with Michael

Stipe, with whom he became close friends in the weeks leading up to his death. Most revealingly, in early 1994 he said, "I hate to actually say it, but I can't see this band lasting more than a couple of albums, unless we really work hard on experimenting. When the same people are together doing the same job, they're limited. I'm really interested in studying different things and I know Dave and Chris are as well, but I don't know if we are capable of doing it together. We are stuck in such a rut. We have been labelled."

First and foremost Cobain was a musician, just as Nirvana were a band. The impact their unprecedented alternative success had, and will have, on the musical landscape of the Nineties and beyond is by far the most important aspect of this sorry saga. The central feature of the whole scenario is the music, above all else the music. It was genuinely seminal, despite accusations of retrogressive parody coming from people for whom the music was never intended in the first instance. Take Cobain's voice – it was like an open, weeping wound, lacerating his emotions, expressing his sad-eyed lyrics that inspired thousands despite their frequently obtuse slant. One moment he would sound as though a demon was trying to rip out his throat, the next he would sing a sweet melody that invited comparisons to Lennon – rarely has there been such a contrast in style in one voice.

In addition, it was unusual that a lyricist so revered should publicise his lack of regard for lyrical content, but Cobain never tried to hide this. "When I write a song, the lyrics are the least important thing," he said. "I can go through two or three different subjects in a song and the title can mean absolutely nothing at all." The desperation and morbidity of the lyrics from 'In Utero' suggested this was being rather modest, as did the evocative response his words provoked among millions of kids. Allied to the lyrical originality and vocal delivery there was always the music – melodious and mellifluous one minute, thundering and gut-wrenching the next, cutting powerful dynamics both live and on record. His intelligent use of pop melodies, often simple and minimalist, over such an awesome background was captivating. When combined, the result was brutal but breathtaking. This was, above all, the fire for Nirvana's success, above corporate scams, marketing devices and plans. It was the most brilliant music for over a decade and that could never be kept underground.

Very few bands are genuinely dangerous, and when reports filtered through that Nirvana were blowing Tad and Mudhoney off stage every night in 1989, this was the word that was being used. They intimidated, they were unsettlingly intense and they

'TEENAGE ANGST HAS PAID OFF WELL, NOW I'M BORED AND OLD' *KURT*

'I TRY EVERY NIGHT, BUT I JUST CAN'T FOOL MYSELF. I'M NOT GOING TO SMILE AND POSE LIKE EDDIE VAN HALEN' *KURT*

had an unpredictable ferocity that fascinated people. They didn't tell jokes (Mudhoney), they were not tongue-in-cheek (Tad) and they were not overt about any musical cross-overs (Red Hot Chilli Peppers and Faith No More). This stern approach set them apart from the Sub Pop label's generic sound and often humorous approach. They delivered the goods with intimidation, but also possessed the ability to screw up badly, such as at the New York Music seminar when previewing 'In Utero', a failing that only added to their appeal.

With 'Nevermind' they had an album that crossed so many genres and which opened up uncharted territories for underground bands. Ironically, Cobain thought 'Teen Spirit' was a cliché on the 'Louie Louie' riff , as did his two colleagues, who thought he was joking when he first played them the song. It took time for the world to wake up to Nirvana among the other contenders, but when it did, it witnessed the birth of a phenomenon.

So it was left for Nirvana to carry the underground flag into the corporate battlefield. In 1991 they overturned years of establishment oppression by clawing their way to the surface as the major bastions fell one by one, breaking dozens of genre barricades along the way. 'Nevermind' represented a seismic shift in attitudes in many ways; in musical fashion, in radio and TV programming, in media prejudices and in record company policies. The only blot on the landscape was that certain elements in Nirvana's own backyard forced them to do too much and in so doing weakened their resolve and enthusiasm. In this respect they could have learned a lesson from Led Zeppelin, whose career took off at the same speed but who deliberately under-exposed themselves thereafter despite corporate pressure.

Nirvana's lofty position was such that during the third album project, the media was already talking up new acts as 'post-Nirvana' (as predicted by Courtney Love) and among the droves of inferior copies there were some genuine new talents arriving in Pavement and Sebadoh.

Cobain himself helped some bands, name-dropping whoever he felt needed recognition whenever possible, an act of generosity that helped him salvage some dignity. The point was that through the massive success of Nirvana, the business and musical landscape of the Nineties was transformed. In essence they achieved the unthinkable: they made the underground popular.

In doing so Nirvana came to capture the zeitgeist of the Nineties, as overnight a generation of kids abandoned previous heroes for a new mentor. Although Cobain never really accepted this role and felt pressured by it (note his remarks about the drug use he feared would influence youngsters), this was an

COBAIN'S OPEN THROATED HAEMORRHAGES ON STAGE
WERE EVEN MORE TORTURED AND CAUSTIC THAN ON RECORD

unavoidable consequence of Nirvana's success. Their influence on the generation was twofold: the band's activism motivated the disparate elements of youth, while the celebrity of Cobain himself inspired equally as many.

The kids who grew up in America in the Eighties were constantly being told that rock and roll had happened, that the real stars and real music had been and gone and they had missed the bus. This arrogant view only exacerbated their frustrations. The Eighties will go down as a selfish decade, when the Reagan administration encouraged a policy which, as in Britain, profited many hundreds of thousands of people, but did nothing to convince or persuade the younger generation. Youth culture in these times was pallid and apathetic, and bands like Guns n'Roses seemed to have little or no political agenda.

For these so-called disenfranchised kids, Nirvana represented a time, a period when this group of society had its own rules, its own leaders, its own ideas. The band liberated the thousands of Aberdeens across America and indeed the world.

Nirvana encouraged the kids to vote, campaigned against the Anti-Erotic Music Bill, played benefit gigs whenever possible, and generally pushed youth to be activist – instead of falling into the apathy of the 'no future' punk ethos. They encouraged kids to fight for their own future. The sincerity with which they did this set them apart from their peers, and millions of kids rallied behind their call to 'be aware'.

Complementing this ability to mobilise a generation was the celebrity of Kurt Cobain himself, which was slightly more based in adoration than lofty cultural considerations. Physically, despite his small frame, he cut a distinctive figure: bespectacled, blond haired and sad eyed with an angel face beaming out all this intensity and emotion. In his strange and unusually attractive eyes there was a self-containment that suggested we would never fully know the private demons that haunted him. He was the angel with the monster inside and it was a compelling mix. When he struck a chord he struck a nerve in the minds of the kids watching him, and they would hurry home to read up on the scandalous stories of drugs, drink, lashing mood swings and anti-stardom.

Every rock star appeals for different reasons – Cobain's adherence to anti-establishment views and feelings of alienation attracted millions of youngsters to relate to him in a very personal way. He was in the multi-million pound music business but here he was, apparently no different from them with the same loneliness, the same anger, the same energy, even the same shirt. When he walked on stage as the meek, cherub faced misfit and launched into a larynx ripping, eye bulging howl, the contrast was fascinating. As he slid into drug abuse the reclusive life he sought merely reinforced his appeal. He was a frail genius who rarely woke before 2pm and had taken to wearing sluttish make-up. As an icon for the Nineties he was perfect, whether he liked it or not.

Twenty years from now Kurt Cobain will be remembered as the greatest songwriter of his generation who died by his own hand. Questions remain about the future for his distraught wife and fatherless child. Amongst his many achievements, this was perhaps Cobain's biggest failure – he had taken on the responsibility of fatherhood and a family and in committing suicide he irrevocably abdicated this most serious of responsibilities. Drug abuse, wild lifestyles and world wide touring are the stuff of rock legends, but that has never been the ideal environment for raising a young child. Love now faces a long struggle against the media and her own guilt over her husband's death and drug problems, so the attentions of the growing child will have much competition. For this reasons Cobain's suicide was undeniably selfish.

He had choices and he made them throughout his life – he chose to leave Aberdeen, to form the band and make his first record. He chose to sign a major deal and knowingly incite the mass media and public interest (admittedly not on the scale he eventually suffered). He chose to marry and start a family, he chose to take the destructive drugs and he could have chosen to stop the band and live off the earnings in a more secluded style.

Ultimately he chose to kill himself. He made those choices and that is one luxury many people can ill afford, financially or otherwise, so do not sympathise with him for these reasons. Suicide is a sad and terrible feature of modern life, but perhaps not as sad as the death of someone who is desperately fighting tooth and nail to stay alive. Nor is his death a major humanitarian loss, when compared to the daily atrocities flashed across our screens. What is absolutely essential here is a sense of perspective – there is one young girl whose only knowledge of her father will be based on the same hearsay and rumour that future Nirvana fans will have to survive on.

Kurt Cobain's life should also not be turned into some macabre suffering of the martyr of a generation. Tradition dictates that rock and roll deaths are often due to overpaid delinquents wanting to live too much, too soon. People like Sid Vicious wanted it all and they wanted it now. Kurt Cobain on the other hand had simply lost the will to live, he did not want to

carry on. It was a sad, wasteful and pointless end for an incredibly talented and gifted man. Deifying him into a new martyr would only cheapen that talent. It was neither surprising nor glamorous that he died as he did – he was part of rock's history of characters who live desperately, so it should not have come as the shock it did.

What is beyond doubt and debate is the musical legacy of Kurt Cobain and Nirvana. He was this generation's most inspirational songwriter, and his work motivated and entertained millions of people across the globe. In so doing, he and his band revolutionised the musical environment of the decade, business and otherwise.

Nirvana proved that the record buying public were not congenitally conservative and were in fact open minded. Their final legacy will only become apparent when the years pass and the long-term effects of the band surface. Maybe the band did not make people think differently, perhaps that flatters them too much, but they certainly effected change, which is the greatest legacy of any band. They articulated a dissatisfaction bubbling under the surface, and by capturing the mood they allowed it to explode. Sadly, with their gigs getting bigger and bigger and communication with their audience already virtually impossible, the band stalled in their own success.

Perhaps the only act of rebellion left to Cobain when he had conquered the American market was to throw it all away. The biggest irony of Nirvana is that rather than being destroyed by convention, they ultimately perished at the hands of the creature they had created to avoid it.

Premature deaths freeze moments and people in time, crystallising forever the passion or the sadness of someone, famous or not. In Kurt Cobain's case, he should be remembered as a brilliant songwriter who took the underground to the mainstream and left a legacy of classic songs behind him. All the rest, the drugs, the love stories, the media frenzy, are distractions from the fact.

Each generation has a right to its own heroes and Cobain, by making his inadequacy a great cathartic roar, was reluctantly one of those. It is not easy being a living legend, and living legends rarely learn to live with it. If Kurt Cobain had been born ten years later in one of the thousands of Aberdeens across the world, and had himself been entranced by the sound of Nirvana, the biggest tragedy for him as a young fan would have been the fact that there would never be another Nirvana record.

IT IS NOT EASY BEING A LIVING LEGEND, AND LIVING LEGENDS RARELY LEARN TO LIVE WITH IT

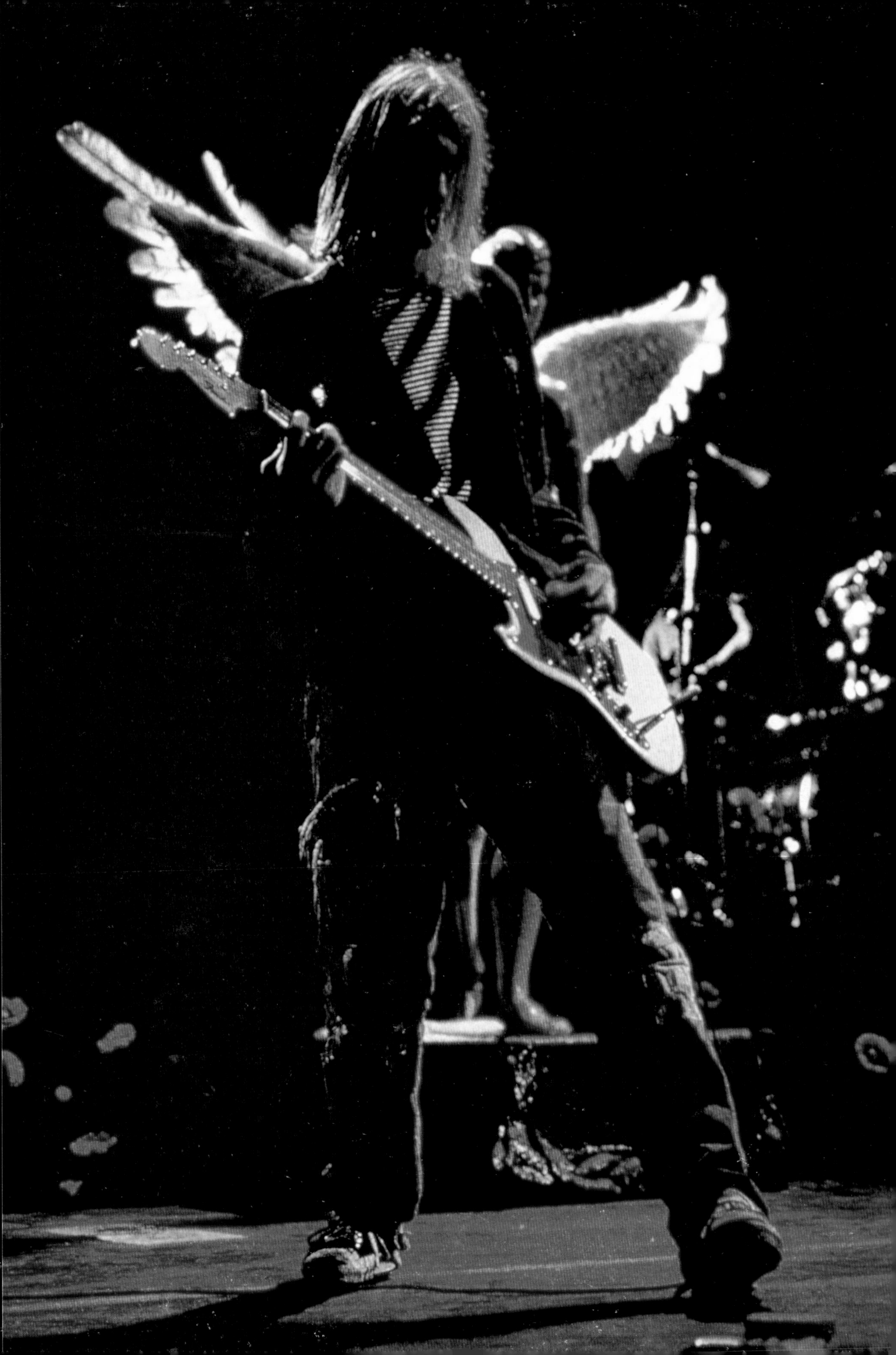

FOR AN INCREDIBLY TALENTED AND GIFTED MAN